465130097

CAST OF CHARACTERS

BARBARA
RANDY
MOTHER
JANE
POKEY

The action of the play takes place during the morning, afternoon, and evening of a Saturday on a July 4th weekend, on the terrace of a large, old summer house, overlooking the sea, on an island off the coast of Massachusetts.

The terrace occupies most of the stage. It is surrounded by a low sitting wall, and contains primarily old terrace furniture, wicker, metal, and wood, thick with many coats of white paint. There is only an occasional concession to aluminum and vinyl. Behind, there is the side of the house, composed of weathered shingles. Ground-floor windows, framed by shutters, graced with window boxes containing geraniums and petunias, open onto the terrace, and of course a large screen door, which slams closed by means of a rusty, sagging spring.

To the left, screened by shrubs, a path leads off and down to the driveway and the tennis court. To the right, around the corner of the house, another path leads to wooden steps down the bluff to the beach.

Notes: Everyone in this play should look thoroughly tanned. The clothes they wear—and they are the kind of people who change their clothes a lot—should be bright, summery, expensive-looking, and conservatively stylish.

The songs should not be considered isolated interludes, but rather should contribute to the flow of the play. They should begin as a scene is ending, and fade out only after the next scene has begun. Similarly the light changes should be carefully modulated.

Finally, the house should be used almost as a character in the play. The upstairs shades should be closed for the first scene. The leafy shadows change over its surface during the day. Before the final scene, the lights come on inside, and for the first time we can see something of the interior.

SYNOPSIS OF SCENES

ACT I:

Scene 1: 7 A.M.

Scene 2: Mid-morning

Scene 3: Late morning

Scene 4: Before lunch.

ACT II:

Scene 1: After lunch

Scene 2: Late afternoon

Scene 3: Early evening

Scene 4: Night

ACT I

*The sound of a group of amateur voices
singing, in good, close, genial harmony, as
if at a beach party:*

You are my sunshine,
    My only sunshine,
You make me happy,
    When skies are gray.
You'll never know, dear,
    How much I love you,
Please don't take my sunshine
            away . . .

*The lights come up on the terrace. It is very
early in the morning. Bright sunlight has
begun to slant across the stage, which will
become brighter as the scene continues.*

*No one is in view. We hear various sounds:
birds chirping off left; the slow pound of the
sea off right. Then, off left, the motor of a
car getting closer, and the crunch of its
wheels on a gravel driveway. The crunch
stops; the motor stops. Car doors are heard
slamming. Then, closer at hand, but still off
left, a Woman giggles. Finally, we can make
out some of her words.*

Woman's voice   Sssshhhh. You'll wake Mother . . . All right, this is far
enough . . . Mmmmmm . . . You'd better go. People
will see you . . . Goodnight—ooops, I mean, good
morning . . .

*Barbara comes on from the left. She is tan,
lean, and attractive, in her late thirties. She
wears a stylish summer outfit which looks
slightly disheveled, as is her hair. She tiptoes
on, carrying her shoes in one hand. Then she
turns back, climbs onto the wall, and waves
down and off left. When the car door slams
again, she cringes and puts her finger to her
lips. She waves as the car is heard driving off.
She sighs and turns toward the house.
Stealthily, she makes her way on tip-toes*

> *toward the screen door. She opens it very carefully, trying not to make its spring squeak. She is about to enter the house when suddenly the strident sound of a telephone is heard ringing within. She starts, jumps back, catches the screen door before it slams shut, and looks around, frightened, at a loss for what to do. The telephone rings two or three times, then stops in the middle of a ring, indicating that someone within has picked up the receiver.*

> *Barbara stands in the center of the terrace. Sounds begin, within the house. First, children's voices, murmuring sleepily and petulantly. Then a Man's voice:*

Man's voice   What the hell was that?

Woman's voice   *(sleepily)* I think it was the telephone. I think your mother answered it.

Man's voice   *(sleepily)* At seven o'clock? Jesus Christ.

> *Barbara, now unable to enter the house with all the noise, sits down resignedly on the wall. Voices continue, adlibbing within. Then, after a moment, the screen door bursts open, and Randy comes out, wrapping a towel around his waist. He is in early thirties, trim, very tan, and athletically built. He calls back into the house as he comes out.*

Randy   I'm going for a swim.

> *He comes onto the terrace, stops short when he sees Barbara.*

Randy   Hey!

Barbara   Good morning.

Randy   You look like you just got home.

Barbara   I did. *(lying)* Betsy's car broke down after the movie, so I stayed over at her house.

Randy   *(believing her)* Oh. *(gesturing toward the house)* Goddam phone woke everybody up.

Barbara   I heard. Who was it?

Randy   I dunno. Mother got it in her bedroom.

Barbara   Probably a wrong number.

Randy	*(stretching; yawning)* No. She's still talking. *(Starts for the right)* I'm going for a swim.
Barbara	No kidding.

> *Randy moves toward the right, then stops, and turns back.*

Randy	Hey, do you know where the oil is?
Barbara	The suntan oil?
Randy	*(irritably)* No, not the suntan oil. The oil for the tennis court roller. I was looking all over for it last night.
Barbara	Did you look in the shed?
Randy	It's not in the shed.
Barbara	It used to be in the shed.
Randy	It's not there, Barbara.
Barbara	Then I don't know where the oil is, Randy.
Randy	*(starting off again)* Christ, you can't find a thing around here. No one puts things back. I don't mind people using things if they put them back.
Barbara	Oh stop trying to be like Daddy.
Randy	*(turning again)* You mean, because I'm taking a dip?
Barbara	No, I mean the lecture about putting things back.
Randy	You never do, and you never did. I have a game this morning, and the court's a mess.
Barbara	*(yawning)* I didn't take the oil, Randy.
Randy	You didn't even put the roller back after Labor Day last year. It was out all winter. That's why it's rusty. That's why I have to oil the damn thing. *(he starts off right again)*
Barbara	Did you ever think that the children might have taken it?
Randy	*(stopping and turning again)* Not my children.
Barbara	Here we go.
Randy	My children put things back. We've trained them.
Barbara	So now you're blaming my children.
Randy	Who lost the pump for the boat?
Barbara	Oh Randy, that's mean.
Randy	Who lost the pump?
Barbara	That's just plain mean. My children are naturally upset,

and you start nit-picking about oil and pumps and
rollers and . . .

Randy   You can't run a house unless people put things back.
         You can't . . .

         *Both are talking at once. The screen door
         opens, and Mother comes out of the house.
         She is in her early sixties, and looks neat and
         well-groomed, in her good-looking bathrobe,
         even at this hour of the morning. Randy and
         Barbara begin to appeal to her immediately
         and simultaneously.*

Barbara Mother, now he's blaming my children because he
         can't find the oil for the tennis court roller . . .

Randy   Mother, I've got a game at ten-thirty and I can't play
         on that court unless I . . .

         *Mother closes her eyes and puts both hands
         over her ears.*

Mother   Ssshhhh.

         Randy and Barbara stop

         Just . . . sshhhh. Let me pull myself together. *(opens
         her eyes)* Guess who just telephoned from the main-
         land?

Barbara Who?

Mother   Guess who will be on the ten o'clock ferry?

Randy   Who, Mother?

Mother   Guess who decided to join us for the Fourth of
         July weekend after all? *(pause)*

Barbara Pokey.

Mother   *(nodding)* Your brother.

Randy   Pokey?

Mother   *(sitting down)* Your little brother. With Miriam. And
         both children. We meet them at eleven-fifteen.

Barbara Well, well.

Mother   They made up their minds *yester*day. Drove all night.
         All the way up from Washington.

Barbara Typical.

Mother   He called from Providence. At seven o'clock in the
         morning. He said he figured we'd all be up.

Barbara	Typical

> *Mother nods, looks at her, suddenly notices her clothes*

Mother	Barbara, where have you been?
Barbara	*(mechanically)* Car broke down. Stayed at Betsy's. Just got in.
Mother	You must be exhausted.
Barbara	*(stretching; yawning)* I am.
Mother	Well, you'll have to stay awake long enough to come to the ferry with me.
Randy	I can't, Mother. I've got a game.
Mother	Oh Randy, you always have a game when I need you. *(She shakes her head, looks out to sea. A pause)*
Barbara	Why is he coming, Mother?
Mother	I suppose because I invited him. Just as I invite both of you. Every year.
Randy	But he refused, Mother. Remember when we called him last Christmas? He showed no interest.
Barbara	He hasn't been near this place in—what?—four years?
Mother	Five.
Barbara	That's right. Ever since Daddy died.
Randy	And now, suddenly, on the spur of the moment . . .
Mother	Well he's changed his mind, that's all. *(Pause; she gets up, squares her shoulders, is now all business)* And of course, I'm delighted. I'm thrilled. We'll all be together for the Fourth. What fun. *(pause)* It just requires some additional planning, that's all. *(She paces around the terrace, counting on her fingers)* Let's see. There's Barbara, and Randy, and Jane, and me, and now Pokey and Miriam. That's six grown-ups. And Barbara's two children, and Randy's four, and Pokey's two. That's eight children. Which means a total of fourteen people in this house. We'll have to get more food on the way to the ferry.
Barbara	And liquor, Mother.
Mother	Oh they won't drink much.
Barbara	No, but we will.

Barbara and Randy laugh

Mother   *(firmly)* There is plenty of liquor, Barbara.

> *Laughter subsides. Mother continues to plan, nervously.*

Now please. Let me think. He'll want his old room, so we'll move all the children out onto the screen porch. Which means changing sheets. Which means stopping at the laundry. And I'll have to get the little MacKenzie girl from down the road to feed the children and help with the dishes. And of course, I've got to come up with his favorite meal tonight. Which means leg of lamb, *and* mint jelly, *and* red raspberries, if I can *find* them, and then there's the Yacht Club dance, and I suppose I should call and make two more reservations, and . . .

Randy   Did he *say* why he decided to come Mother?

> *Pause; Mother looks at him*

Mother   No. He didn't say . . . *(She sits pensively)*

Barbara   He avoids us like the plague for five years, and then suddenly . . .

Randy   Oh he's always doing this. Remember the time he ran away from summer camp? And just arrived, on the doorstep, in the middle of a party?

Barbara   I remember the time he *left*. Remember that, Mother? You were having some people over for him, and right before they arrived, he walked in with his knapsack packed and said he was hitch-hiking out west? And that was before hitch-hiking was even fashionable!

Randy   I thought he'd settle down, now he's married. Do you think he's quit his job again, Mother?

Mother   He didn't say . . . *(pause. Mother stands up)* But I know. I know why he's coming. He's coming because of my letter.

Randy   Your—letter?

Mother   My letter. People still write letters, Randy. Occasionally. When they want to say things that can't be said on the telephone. When they want to have things sink in. That's when they write letters. *(pause)* And knowing the United States mail, your brother just got that letter yesterday. And apparently it *didn't* sink in. It didn't sink in at all. Because he throws his poor wife and children into the car, and drives all night, and doesn't call until he's practically *here,* so that we can't say no, we can't say relax, we can't say please, before you come, at least let it sink *in. (pause)* That's why he's coming. *(pause)*

Barbara   What did the letter say, Mother? *(pause)*

Mother   Well first, I said we'd all miss him, and I wished them all a very happy Fourth of July.

Barbara   And?

Mother   And then I asked him to do some serious thinking about the fall.

Randy   The fall?

Mother   The fall. Because in the fall—as I wrote your brother—you three children will get this house.

Barbara   But—why, Mother?

Mother   *(taking a deep breath)* Because in the fall, in September, to be exact—now this is a secret. Nobody knows about this—*(pause)* In the fall, in September, your Uncle Bill and I are going to get married. *(She turns and strides into the house)*

                        Pause. Barbara and Randy look at each other.

Barbara   Wow.

Randy   *(looking toward the house)* She told him first. Why does she always tell him things first?

                        Pause. They look at each other again, and then of one accord rush into the house after their Mother, calling, That's great, Mother!; That's terrific; Why didn't you tell us? *etc.*

                        The lights dim as we hear congratulations within.

                        The Group of Voices sings:

                        I want a girl
                            Just like the girl
                                That married dear old Dad . . .

                        She was a pearl,
                            And the only girl
                                That Daddy ever had . . .

                        The good old-fashioned kind with heart so true . . .
                        The kind that loves nobody else but you . . .

*The Song fades as the lights have come up
again*

*The brightness of the overhead sun indicates
that it is about eleven-thirty in the morning.
After a moment, Jane comes out of the house,
a pretty woman in her mid-thirties. She
wears a white tennis dress, white hair band,
and white sneakers. She carries a tray with
two glasses of coke on it, which she puts on a
table. Then she calls toward off left*

Jane   I'm out here, Randy.

*Pause. Then Randy comes on from around the
house, now also in whites. He carries a tennis
raquet. He glances at Jane, then walks to the
edge of the sitting wall. He hauls off, about
to hurl the raquet away*

Oh don't, Randy! That's a new raquet.

*He looks at the raquet, shakes his head, and
tosses it aside. He slumps angrily into a chair.
Jane brings him a coke.*

We should have gone to the ferry with everyone else.

Randy   We had a game.

Jane   Some game.

Randy   All right. I stank.

Jane   You got so mad.

Randy   They never knew. We shook hands, and all that.

Jane   They didn't even stay for a coke.

Randy   They couldn't, Jane. They had to get back to their
            children.

Jane   They *said* they had to get back to their children.
            Who are in camp.

Randy looks at her. Pause.

I love the ferry. All that kissing and hugging.

Randy   Pokey and I don't hug.

Pause. They sip their cokes.

You know why we lost?

Jane   You got mad.

Randy   You know why I got mad?

Jane	You're upset about your mother.
Randy	Not at all.
Jane	It makes sense, psychologically.
Randy	I said, not at *all*, Jane.
Jane	I mean, you're very close to her. You don't want to see her go.
Randy	She's not *go*ing anywhere. She'll be right here, every summer. With all of us. And Uncle Bill. Who's a great old friend of the family. Who was one of Daddy's ushers in their wedding, for God's sake. It's perfect. It's ideal.
Jane	I think so, too.
Randy	So that's not why I got mad.
Jane	All right.
Randy	That's not why we lost.
Jane	All right, dear.

Long pause; They both look out to sea.

Randy	You want to know why we lost?
Jane	Because of Pokey.
Randy	No.
Jane	Well you say he always makes you nervous.
Randy	He's not the reason.
Jane	Well you're always saying that. Everybody says it. Isn't that why you all call him Pokey? Because he's always poking around, making everybody nervous?
Randy	We call him Pokey because he has a poker face.
Jane	Oh.
Randy	And because he was a slow-poke. He was always holding us up.
Jane	Your mother said it was because he liked to poke around. I remember, because she said he now has the perfect job. In Washington. Working for the Department of Justice. She said now he can poke around the entire country, stirring things up.
Randy	Oh maybe . . .
Jane	I'm sure she said that. She said that both her sons had perfect jobs. You teaching at a boys' boarding school because you love sports and games, and Pokey poking around for the Department of Justice.

Randy	O.K., O.K.
Jane	So probably you were nervous about Pokey on the tennis court.
Randy	Wrong.
Jane	O.K.
Randy	Just plain wrong, Jane.
Jane	O.K. Skip it.

Pause. They look out to sea again.

Randy	You want to know why we lost? Really?
Jane	I still think . . .
Randy	Do you want to know why?
Jane	It's your mother. Or Pokey. Or both. I'll bet you.
Randy	*(shouting)* DO YOU WANT TO KNOW WHY WE LOST THAT GODDAM GAME OF TENNIS, JANE? *(pause)*
Jane	Why?
Randy	Because of the court.
Jane	The court? What's wrong with the court?
Randy	What's wrong with the *court*? What's wrong with that tennis court, out there? I'll tell you what's wrong with the court. Everything's wrong with the court. You can't see the lines, the net is riddled with holes, the surface is like a battlefield. How can a man play under those conditions? How can a man who is used to a decent court play on a court like that? Daddy wouldn't have played. Daddy would have walked right off that court. I tell the kids, I tell the boys at school, there's no point in playing a game unless you have good equipment. A man's got to be able to count on certain fundamental *things*. It's like Latin. That's why I like Latin. When I'm teaching Latin, I say look for the verb. You can always count on the verb. Find the verb, and everything will fall into place. Now maybe those clods we played tennis with today don't care about these things. Maybe they're used to bad bounces, and foot faults, and wrong scores.
Jane	The score wasn't wrong.
Randy	He called it wrong. Twice. I had to correct him. Because I care about the score. And I care about lines and nets and smooth surfaces and bounces that I can

at least pre*dict*. And that's why we lost, if you really want to know. *(pause)*

Jane   All right. *(pause)*

Randy   And I'll tell you something else. We're going to resurface that court. That's the first thing. That's first on the list, when the house is ours.

Jane   I think Barbara wants to winterize the house. She's always talking about it.

Randy   Well the court comes first. *(pause)*

Jane   Would you explain something to me, please?

Randy   What?

Jane   Why do you get the house when your mother gets married?

Randy   It was in Daddy's will.

Jane   Oh.

Randy   It's in most wills.

Jane   Oh.

Randy   The house is in the wife's name until she dies or remarries. Then it goes to the children. It's standard practice.

Jane   Oh. And Pokey understands all that?

Randy   Of course he does. He's the executor of the will.

Jane   Oh then that explains it.

Randy   Explains what?

Jane   Why he's suddenly coming up. To handle these legal things.

Randy   I suppose.

Jane   Oh that's a relief. You know what I thought?

Randy   What?

Jane   I thought he was upset about your mother.

Randy   *(exploding)* JESUS, JANE—

          A car horn is heard off left. Car doors
          slamming, the sound of children's voices.

Jane   Well. There they are. *(She gets up)*

Randy   *(getting up)* So let's get Pokey to chip in on the court, O.K.?

Jane   *(moving toward the left)* Does he still play?

Randy   Of course he does. He's quite good.

                     Jane is almost out

             But I can beat him.

                     Jane is out left by now. Randy follows her,
                     calling after her.

             I can beat him easily.

                     He is shouting after her as he
                     goes.

             Even on that crumby court, with those lousy lines,
             and that stringy net between us, I can still beat him.
             Ask Mother. Mother will tell you. I can slaughter him.

                     He is off left by now, as the
                     lights dim.

                     SONG:

                     . . . For all the world is sad and dreary,
                             Everywhere I roam,
                         O, darling, how my heart grows weary,
                             Far from the old folks at home . . .

                     The lights are up by now. It is high noon. The
                     sound of children's voices can be heard
                     occasionally offstage.

                     Mother comes out of the house, now dressed in
                     colorful slacks and blouse. She sits on the wall,
                     looking out to sea. Then Barbara comes out, in
                     a change of clothes, carrying a gin-and-tonic.
                     She looks at her Mother.

Barbara   Well. He's changing.
Mother   *(with a sigh)* Do you think so?
Barbara   His clothes, Mother. He's changing his clothes.
Mother   Oh.
Barbara   Thank God he's getting out of that dark suit. He
             looked like a visiting minister.
Mother   *(glancing toward the house)* Sssshhhh. *(pause)*
Barbara   *(lower voice)* What did you think of *her* outfit?
Mother   Miriam? She's sweet.
Barbara   Her *out*fit. Mother. What did you think of that little
             number?
Mother   I thought it was very pretty.
Barbara   Oh Mother . . .

Mother	Very snappy.
Barbara	Snappy? That halter job? And no *bra*, Mother?
Mother	That's the style these days. *(pause)* Apparently. *(pause)*
Barbara	What about the children? How did you like them getting off the ferry in their grubby little blue jeans?
Mother	Styles change, Barbara.
Barbara	Oh do they? I don't see you giving my children blue jeans for Christmas. It seems to me I remember nice little boxes from Saks Fifth Avenue.
Mother	People live different lives, Barbara.
Barbara	They certainly do. He looks like a relic from the Eisenhower age escorting a bunch of hippies around.
Mother	That's enough, please.
Barbara	And pale. Don't they allow the sun down in Washington? Is that one of their new laws?
Mother	They'll get the sun here.
Barbara	Let's hope so. Can you imagine us all cooped up here together on a rainy day?

Pause. Mother shakes her head

Mother	The first thing he did when he got here, the first thing, he walked right out on this terrace, and looked at the view, and said, "Where's the rose garden? Where's the old croquet court?" So I said, "Erosion, dear. Natural erosion. You just haven't been here."
Barbara	If there's erosion, Pokey would notice it.
Mother	He says we need a sea-wall.
Barbara	Oh my God, that costs a fortune.
Mother	That's what he says. Otherwise, he says some night we're going to be sitting here drinking, and the whole house will slide slowly into the sea.
Barbara	Pokey, Pokey, Pokey . . .
Mother	*(with a sigh)* Well, we've just got to loosen him up, that's all.
Barbara	How? How do we loosen up Pokey?
Mother	By being very affectionate and warm-hearted.

Barbara laughs; Mother looks at her

	What's so funny?
Barbara	The way we were at the ferry?
Mother	What was wrong at the ferry?

Barbara	Nothing. We were all on our best behavior.
Mother	We welcomed him with open arms.
Barbara	A peck for a kiss.
Mother	I didn't peck.
Barbara	We both pecked, Mother. And the children shook hands.
Mother	Well what should we have done? Are we supposed to fall all over each other, like that Italian family?
Barbara	Not at all. We're not the type. *(pause)* Except maybe Pokey. Remember how he cried at Daddy's funeral?
Mother	We all cried.
Barbara	But no so *much*. God, tears were streaming down his face. The rest of us were good old undemonstrative Wasps.
Mother	I hate that expression, Wasp. Everyone uses it these days, and I loathe it.
Barbara	It's what we are, Mother.
Mother	We are not. We are people, like Italians or anybody else. We love our family, and we're very affectionate when we're not in public. *Hon*estly. *(pause)* We all cried. *(pause)* I don't like all this smart talk, Barbara. I know you're upset about your divorce, but I don't want to see you turning into a bitter, disagreeable woman. Now you'd better learn to be nice to both your brothers, because you're all going to take over in the fall. *(pause. She looks out to sea)*
Barbara	What's the matter, Mother?
Mother	Nothing's the matter. *(pause)* Except that he never even mentioned my getting married.
Barbara	No kidding.
Mother	Not a word. Not at the ferry, not in the car, not out here, not at all.
Barbara	No kidding. *(pause)*
Mother	*(carefully)* I suppose he mentioned it to you.
Barbara	No.
Mother	You must have brought it up.
Barbara	I tried. At one point.
Mother	What did you say?
Barbara	Oh I said, "What do you think of the good news, Pokey?" Something like that.

Mother   What did he say?

Barbara   Nothing. He walked away.

            Mother sighs

            He was fussing with his children. *(pause)*

Mother   The only way it came up with me was when I told him
            we were having his favorite meal tonight. Do you know
            what he said? He said, "I hope it's just the family."
            That's all he said. *(pause)* Well. Just the family it will
            be.

Barbara   Not Uncle Bill?

            Mother shakes her head

            Oh Mother, we were going to have toasts. And sing
            songs. I got some wine.

            Mother shakes her head

            Uncle Bill's part of the family.

Mother   Not to Pokey. Pokey won't even call him Uncle Bill.

Barbara   We've always called him Uncle Bill.

Mother   Pokey hasn't. He calls him Mister. He used to say that
            Uncle Bill's not his uncle, so why should he call him
            that. *(pause)* Pokey doesn't like him.

Barbara   Oh Mother.

Mother   He doesn't like him. He can be very rude to him. I've
            seen it. *(pause)* That's why I wrote him that letter. So
            he could get used to the idea. *(pause)* I told Pokey
            first. Before I told any of you. Uncle Bill hasn't even
            told *his* children yet. But I thought I should tell Pokey.
            (pause) So. No Uncle Bill for dinner. No celebration.
            Just the family. *(She gets up, smiles, squares her
            shoulders)* And maybe it's just as well. Aunt Peggy just
            died in March. We shouldn't be jumping the gun,
            should we? To be fair to her. So maybe it's just as
            well if we all just avoided the issue for the weekend,
            and had a nice family dinner, and then we'll see Uncle
            Bill at the Yacht Club dance. *(She starts for the house)*
            And now I think I'll take a bath before lunch.

            Barbara laughs. Mother turns

            Now what's so funny?

Barbara   Oh Mother . . .

Mother   What's wrong with taking a bath?

Barbara   Nothing's *wrong* with it. But have you noticed that

	since Pokey arrived, everyone makes a dash for the water.
Mother	Phooey.
Barbara	It's true. I went in, Jane went in, the children went in, Randy's still in, and now you're making a bee-line for the bathtub.
Mother	It's a hot day.
Barbara	Oh sure.
Mother	What's wrong with people keeping clean?
Barbara	Nothing's *wrong,* Mother. It's just who we are. I think that's why we have to be near the ocean. We have to go through these ritual cleansings.
Mother	People feel hot, people feel dirty . . .
Barbara	And people feel guilty. *(pause)*
Mother	Guilty? Guilty about what?
Barbara	Oh lots of things. Money. Having this place when poor people are sweltering in the city. Living off the stock market. All that.
Mother	That's ridiculous.
Barbara	I feel guilty.
Mother	I don't, at all.
Barbara	I do. I feel guilty about my divorce. I feel guilty about— *(She glances toward off left. Pause)* And Pokey always makes me feel more guilty.
Mother	I have nothing to feel guilty about, thank you very much. *(She starts toward the house again)*
Barbara	Maybe you do, and don't even know it.

Mother turns

Face it, Mother. That's who we are. We're very repressive people. That's what my psychiatrist said. We survive on repression. That's how we made our money, and that's how we've held onto it. We hold onto things. We hold on. That's our whole bag. And it's time we realized it.

Mother snorts, strides to the door, opens it, then turns

| Mother | I'll tell *you* what it's time we realized. It's time we realized when to drink and when not to drink. I've noticed that glass in your hand, Barbara, and I haven't |

mentioned it, but now I think it's time I did. I don't like drinking at this hour, and I don't like drinking alone. We have rules about drinking in this house. If your father were alive, he'd make you pour that out. You children are much too casual about alcohol. It's not a toy. *That's* what it's time you realized, frankly, if you want my opinion. *(She goes into the house. The screen door slams behind her.)*

> *Barbara looks after her, looks at the drink in her hand, shakes her head, settles into her chair, takes a long sip.*

Barbara Oh Pokey, Pokey, Pokey. Welcome home . . .

> *The lights dim as we hear:*
> SONG:

Heart of my Heart,
  I love that melody.
Heart of my Heart
  Brings back sweet memories . . .

When we were kids,
  On the corner of the street,
We were rough and ready guys,
  But oh, how we could harmonize . . .

> *The lights are up again. It is about an hour later. Barbara is sound asleep in her chair, her feet up on the wall, her empty glass beside her. Jane comes out of the house, now also dressed in a fresh blouse and slacks.*

Jane *(Not seeing that Barbara is asleep)* There's a slight problem with the children.

Barbara *(starting; sitting up)* What?

Jane Oh I'm sorry.

Barbara That's all right. I had a late night. What's the matter?

Jane The children. They're using four-letter words.

Barbara How did that start?

Jane I'm afraid with Pokey's children.

Barbara Wouldn't you know . . .

Jane They just started in saying them. Every word in the book. And the other children took them up. And now four-letter words are being tossed around the infield, over the peanut-butter sandwiches, amid gales of laughter.

Barbara   Did you stop it?

Jane   Oh I tried to. But then I started to laugh. That didn't help much.

Barbara   Oh Jane . . .

Jane   It was so funny. At one point, it was like a chant. All the most repulsive words. Even the sitter was doing it. I found myself roaring with laughter. *(She laughs; then checks herself)* I hope your mother didn't hear.

Barbara   She's taking a bath.

Jane   Whew. *(She sits down)* Another problem. Pokey's children call me by my first name.

Barbara   Did you ask them to?

Jane   Nope.

Barbara   I think that might be a little fresh, don't you?

Jane   I sort of like it.

Barbara   Then what's the problem?

Jane   Well now your children want to do it.

Barbara   Out of the question.

Jane   Otherwise they say it's not fair.

Barbara   They weren't brought up that way.

Jane   I told them they could.

Barbara   I'll tell them later they can't. *(pause)* Next thing you know, your own children will be calling you Randy and Jane.

Jane   That's what they want to do.

Barbara   You said no, I hope.

Jane   Oh it wouldn't kill me.

Barbara   Randy would kill *them.*

Jane   *(nodding)* I said that. *(pause)* So they'll continue to call me Mummy. *(She shakes her head.)* I hate being called Mummy. I wish I were called Ma. Or Mama Mia. Or just plain old Mom. *(pause)* Not Mummy. It reminds me of all those types I went to boarding school with. They called their Mothers Mummy, and when they wrote, everything slanted backwards, and they dotted their i's with great, big, empty circles.

Barbara   I slant backwards.

Jane	*(sadly)* So do I. *(pause)* It's hard to change. *(pause)* Oh. Remind me to pick up some more coke this afternoon.
Barbara	There's plenty of coke.
Jane	There was.
Barbara	Mother just got coke. This morning.
Jane	They've been through two big bottles.
Barbara	Who?
Jane	The children. Just now.
Barbara	Coke with meals? Mother planned milk.
Jane	Pokey's kids wanted Coca-Cola. So the sitter gave it to them.
Barbara	Are mine having coke? Are yours?
Jane	We had to be fair.
Barbara	Coke is for people who play tennis. That's the rule.
Jane	Maybe it's a Jewish thing.
Barbara	Coke? Coke is Jewish?
Jane	No, the idea of no milk with meals. Maybe it comes from Miriam. Maybe it's a Jewish rule.
Barbara	We have our own rules around here. And one of them is coke is for people who exercise. Think of their *teeth*. I'll tell the sitter.

> *Randy comes in from the right.*
> *He wears a white monogrammed terry-cloth*
> *bathrobe which is a little too big for him. His*
> *hair is wet from swimming. Barbara sees him,*
> *gasps*

Barbara	Oh my God!
Randy	What?
Barbara	That bathrobe! I thought you were Daddy.
Randy	Pokey gave it to me this morning.
Barbara	You'd better get it off before Mother sees it.
Jane	Why?
Barbara	Daddy wore it the day he drowned. She found it on the beach.
Randy	I think she'd want me to wear it.
Barbara	When she's getting married again?

Randy   Pokey said that doesn't mean she wants to forget
             Daddy.

Barbara   *(shaking her head)* I want to forget Fred. I can tell
             you that.

Randy   That's a little different.

Barbara   I'll say.

Randy   Oh. Pokey brought a present for you.

Barbara   Something of Daddy's?

Randy   Yep. He held onto a lot of his stuff.

Barbara   *(getting up)* I'll go see. *(She goes into the house)*

Randy   *(to Jane)* Do you think she'd mind?

Jane   Your mother? I don't know.

Randy   Why should she ? She gave me lots of his sport coats.

Jane   That might be a little big for you.

Randy   It's supposed to be. You're supposed to feel free in it.
             Daddy would wear all these tight, stuffy clothes, but
             when he went swimming, this was it. Mother would try
             to get him to wear a bathing suit when you were around,
             but he wouldn't do it. He said that swimming was the
             one time he wanted to feel absolutely free. Remember?
             He'd roll around the water like an old walrus. *(He shakes
             his head)* I'm the same way. *(He looks at Jane)* You
             look great. New outfit?

Jane   Your mother got it for me in the village.

Randy   I like it.

Jane   You do?

Randy   Don't you?

Jane   I don't know. I thought I did. But now . . .

Randy   What?

Jane   I don't know. After seeing Miriam, I feel so . . .
             square.

Randy   You look great to me.

Jane   It makes me feel like your mother.

Randy   What's wrong with that?

Jane   I don't know. Here I am in your mother's outfit, and
             you're in your father's bathrobe, and we're living in
             your family's house . . . *(She shakes her head)* I don't
             know. *(She walks to the edge of the wall and looks out.)*
                     Randy watches her, then smiles, and comes

	to her. He begins fiddling with the back of her blouse.
Randy	Then let's take it off.
Jane	*(giggling)* Oh Randy, stop it.
Randy	*(nuzzling her)* How about it? A quickie? A little nooner, before lunch? Mmmm? Mmmm?
Jane	*(laughing)* What's come over you?
Randy	*(opening his bathrobe)* This. Look. No hands.
Jane	*(walking away; laughing)* You're repulsive!

> *Randy follows her around. Barbara comes out of the house, carrying a wrist watch.*

Barbara	*(holding it out)* Look what Pokey gave me. Daddy's watch.
Randy	Hey!
Barbara	Daddy left this on the beach, too. *(she shakes it)* It's all rusty. *(she looks at it fondly)* Oh boy. I can remember this. *(Imitating her father)* Barbara, I want you in this house by ten-thirty. No and's, if's, or but's. I intend to be looking at my watch. *(pause)* Pokey kept it. *(pause)* I said, "Pokey, don't you want any of these things? What are you keeping for yourself?"
Randy	What did he say?
Barbara	Nothing. *(pause, She sighs; settles back into her chair)* Well. Anyway, while I was in there, I laid down the law. Milk for everyone. No exceptions. And I told our little teenage townie to take them all out to the meadow for soft-ball as soon as they've finished their ice-cream. No children on this terrace. This is absolutely sancta-sanctorum for grown ups.

> *Randy has begun to nuzzle Jane again*

Oh God, Randy, stop *paw*ing the woman. It's embarrassing, Mother says you do it even in restaurants in New York. Cut it out. What are other people supposed to do when you're doing that?

Randy	Masturbate.
Barbara	Oh Jesus.

> *She looks at the watch fondly, tries to shake it into running. Randy continues to nuzzle*

> *Jane. Then, Barbara seems to make up her*
> *mind, and puts the watch down on the table,*
> *where it stays, in full view, till the end of the*
> *play.*

Randy, do you think you could possibly control
yourself long enough for us to have a small, serious
conversation before Mother and Pokey come down for
lunch?

Randy	Sure.
Barbara	Good

> *She smiles icily; He smiles back*

Do you know, for example, that when Mother
gets married, the house goes to us?

Randy	I know that.
Barbara	Good. *(another smile)* Do you know, also, that I am seriously considering giving up my apartment in Boston, and living down here over the winter?
Randy	Mother doesn't think . . .
Barbara	Mother will be *out* of it, Randy! Now I want to do it, and all I need is a small gas furnace to take care of the bottom floor of the house.
Randy	We need lots of things.
Barbara	We need that first, Randy. Now I've looked around, and I know I can get one put in for a song.
Randy	We need a new tennis court.
Barbara	Will you let me *fin*ish, Randy? Please. I can get one put in for about two thousand dollars.
Randy	Two thousand!
Barbara	That's a bargain, Randy. I've found a builder who will do it almost at cost.
Randy	We could resurface the court for . . .
Barbara	You'll *get* your court, Randy. Next year. Chip in with me for the furnace now, and next year I'll chip in with you on the court! O.K.? *(pause)*
Randy	A thousand? Now? I don't have that kind of money.
Barbara	Oh yes you do.
Randy	Do you know what they pay me at Saint Luke's School?
Barbara	Do you know what I pay for rent in Boston? Do you know what Fred gives me for alimony? We've got to get together on this, Randy.

Randy   I can't afford a thousand.

Barbara   You can, Randy. You know damn well you can. You have your stocks, and Jane is privately endowed . . .

Jane   Oh . . .

Barbara   You are, Jane, and both of you manage to keep four children in private school, and get them on skiis every winter. You can damn well pay for a dinky little furnace, if you wanted to. And you could use it, Randy. You could all come down here. Thanksgiving. And Christmas. We'd all get together. You'd use it more than I'd ever use that court. I mean, what's more important? A home, warmth, shelter—or a goddam game?

Randy   You've got a home.

Barbara   I don't, Randy. I hate Boston. Everyone there is either a professor or a politician. Or both. It's all very moral and earnest, and I hate it, and I want to be here.

Randy   Mother says you'd last about a week.

Barbara   I won't, I swear. I'll send the kids to the local schools, and I'll do some writing . . .

Randy   Writing?

Barbara   Children's books. I want to write children's books. I've always wanted to do that. Always.

Randy   You'd go stir-crazy, sitting around, writing about bunnies, with nobody to see.

Barbara   I'd see people.

Randy   Who? Old ladies? Townies?

Barbara   There are people.

Randy   Who? You'd never go out, Barb.

Barbara   I went out last night.

Randy   With Betsy. To the movies.

Barbara   *(blurting it out)* Says who?

Randy   Says you. You said so. *(pause)*

Barbara   Well maybe I had a date last night. What do you think of that? *(pause)*

Randy   Who with?

Barbara   Never you mind. *(pause)*

Randy   Someone who's going to be around all winter?

Barbara   Maybe. *(pause)*

Randy	Who?
Barbara	That's for me to know.
Randy	Come on. Who?
Barbara	None of your beeswax.
Randy	And you want me to kick in a thousand bucks for some demon lover? *(pause)*
Barbara	Promise you won't tell Mother?
Randy	O.K.
Barbara	Will you chip in on the furnace?
Randy	Maybe. It depends.

Pause. Barbara thinks it over.
Finally:

Barbara	Artie. *(pause)*
Randy	Artie? Artie who? Artie . . . GRIEBER?
Barbara	*(quietly)* Artie Grieber.

pause; Randy whistles

Jane	Who's Artie Grieber?
Randy	Oh my God.
Jane	Who's Artie Grieber?
Randy	He used to cut the *grass* around here.
Barbara	He's a builder now.
Randy	He cut the grass.
Barbara	He's done very well on the island.
Randy	I thought he was married. I thought he had kids.
Barbara	He's getting separated.
Randy	Artie Grieber . . . *(to Jane)* She had a crush on him twenty years ago. *(to Barbara)* Didn't Pokey catch you with him in the maid's room?
Barbara	Pokey caught you doing a few things too, kid.
Randy	*(shaking his head)* Artie Grieber. All night, with Artie Grieber.
Barbara	If you tell Mother, Randy, I swear I'll strangle you.
Randy	Oh my God, I wouldn't dare tell Mother. *(He sits down)* Artie Grieber.
Jane	Is it serious, Barbara?
Barbara	Sort of.
Jane	Do you think you might marry him?

Barbara   Maybe. I . . . see a lot of him. I'm seeing him this
           afternoon.

Randy   *(still shaking his head)* Artie Grieber . . . Old Artie the
           grass-cutter . . . *(he laughs)* So you want to be here in
           the winter, and have Artie come in and turn on your
           furnace, eh?

Barbara   *(angrily)* CUT IT OUT!

                   *Controlling herself, as he continues to
                   chuckle*

           He does tennis courts, Randy. He could put in a whole
           new tennis court for you, next year, at half the cost.
           You get your court, and I get a place to live. Please,
           Randy. I want this. This is very important to me. Can
           we get together on this, please?

                   *Randy looks at her, stops laughing, stands
                   up, wraps his bathrobe tightly around him*

Randy   Who do you think I am? Do you think I'd go along
           with the idea of my sister shacking up all winter in this
           house with Artie Grieber? Jesus, Barbara. Grow up.
           (pause)

Barbara   *(grimly; quietly)* Do you know what a Wasp is, Randy?

Randy   Yes I know what a Wasp is.

Barbara   I don't think you do. So I'll tell you. Because you are
           one. A Wasp is a white Anglo-Saxon prick.

Randy   Big joke.

Barbara   And I'll tell you something else, brother. I'm going to
           be here this winter. I'm going to be right here. You
           wait, buster. You just wait.

Jane   *(looking toward the house)* Ssshhh. Your mother.

                   *A noise within. Then Mother comes out of
                   the house, in different clothes again. She
                   stands at the door, and notices Randy's
                   bathrobe immediately*

Mother   Pokey gave you that.

Randy   Yes, Mother

Mother   *(nodding; turning to Barbara)* And what did he give you?

Barbara   *(indicating the watch on the table)* Daddy's old wrist
           watch.

                   Mother nods and sits down

Mother	I wonder what he brought for me. *(pause)*
Randy	Do you mind, Mother? My wearing this?
Mother	*(brightly)* Mind? Mind? Why should I mind? *(She looks him up and down)* It doesn't fit at *all,* but why should I mind? *(to Barbara)* And the watch, of course, doesn't work. *(pause)* Pokey asked, he specifically asked for both those things when we were going over your father's possessions.
Barbara	Why did he give them to us, then, Mother?
Mother	*(grimly)* I think I can answer that. *(pause)* I've just had a long talk with your brother. *(pause)* Through the bathroom door. While I was taking my bath. *(pause)* In *fact* . . . *(pause)* I think we should all have a drink before lunch. *(a glance at Barbara)* Or another drink, in some cases. *(to Randy)* Randy, go make Bloody Marys. Barbara, there's some Brie left. Get that, and some of those Bremner wafers.
Barbara	What did he *say*, Mother?
Mother	I will tell you when we all have a drink in our hands. Go on, Randy . . . And get into some clothes while you're doing it, please.

> *Randy and Barbara look at her and then go quickly into the house. Jane remains.*
>
> *Pause. Mother looks out to sea, then turns to her with a sigh*

	You and I are going to have to work very hard this weekend, Jane. Very hard indeed. We've got a big job on our hands . . .*(She shakes her head)* Just keeping things going.
Jane	What do you mean?
Mother	*(shaking her head again)* Wait till the others get back. *(pause)* One thing we talked about, Pokey and I, was that outfit you're wearing.
Jane	This?
Mother	That. We talked about that for a while.
Jane	I don't—
Mother	He said it was unfair.
Jane	Unfair?

Mother	Unfair for me to buy you that, and unfair for me to buy Barbara her yellow sweater, when I didn't buy Miriam anything.
Jane	Oh. *(pause)*
Mother	You didn't tell him I bought it, did you?
Jane	No.
Mother	Of course you didn't. He just knows these things. By instinct. Always has. He can sniff out an issue like this a mile away. At Christmas, he could tell if he was one present short without even counting. *(sighs; shakes her head)* Pokey, Pokey, Pokey. *(pause)* So. I said I bought you that outfit because you needed one. Because you and Randy don't have much money. Because Randy just teaches school. And I said I bought Barbara that yellow sweater because Fred just gives her a pittance for alimony. And I said of course I would have bought Miriam something, but she wasn't here, and I don't dare buy her things when she's not here because I never know what she likes.
Jane	That seems fair.
Mother	And I said, all right. This afternoon, I'll take Miriam into the village, and she can buy whatever she wants. On me.
Jane	Did that do it?
Mother	No, I don't think so. All I got from that was silence, on the other side of the bathroom door. *(Pause)* There's always one. In every family. Always one child who behaves like this. Does one of yours always stir things up, Jane?
Jane	Yes.
Mother	Who? Which one? *(Pause)*
Jane	I won't tell.
Mother	*(smiling)* Good. Good for you. *(pause)* But in some ways, don't you love that one most of all?
Jane	Yes. *(pause)*
Mother	Even though it's so exhausting, even though it wears you down, even though you spend more time thinking about that one than any of the others . . . there's a special feeling, isn't there?
Jane	Yes.

Pause. They both look out to sea

Mother   Aaaanyway, that was the first thing we talked about,
            Pokey and I, while I was trying to take a bath, after a
            very long morning, when he hasn't been here in five
            years. That was just the first thing.

Jane   Didn't he talk about your getting married again?

Mother   *(laughing, ironically)* He didn't. So I did. Finally. I
            said, "Pokey, sweetheart, I'm getting *married* in the
            fall. I wrote you a letter, and you haven't even
            mentioned it. Don't you at least want to congratulate
            your mother? Isn't that just a little bit more important
            than who bought what for whom? Kind of? Maybe?
            Sort of? Hmmm?"

Jane   And what did he say?

Mother   Nothing.

Jane   Nothing?

Mother   Nothing. There was more silence. Endless silence. An
            eternity of silence.

Jane   Maybe he didn't hear.

Mother   Oh he heard all right. Because then suddenly he
            launched into the *big* topic of discussion, and—

            *Noise from the house; clinking
            of glasses and ice*

And here, thank heavens, comes something to drink.

            *Randy enters, now in a polo shirt and
            khakis, carrying a tray of glasses and a
            pitcher of Bloody Marys. Barbara follows him
            with a platter of crackers and cheese. As the
            scene continues, Randy hands around the
            drinks, with the appropriate ad-libs. Barbara
            puts the crackers and cheese in front of her
            Mother, who cuts it, puts the cheese on the
            crackers, and hands them out during the
            conversation.*

Mother   Where is Pokey now?

Randy   With his children.

Mother   That's so we can talk it over.

Barbara   Talk *what over?*

            Randy hands his Mother a drink

Mother	Thank you, dear. *(she takes a long sip)* Pokey wants you two to buy him out. *(startled pause)*
Randy	Buy him *out*?
Mother	That's what he said. Buy out his third of the house. In the fall. When it goes to you. When I get married . . . Have some cheese, Jane?

She hands Jane a cracker and cheese

Barbara	He doesn't want it?
Mother	He wants his equity. That's what he says . . . Here, Barbara. Cheese. *(pause)*
Randy	Well . . . O.K. . . .
Mother	O.K.? O.K.? Randy, my dear love, *think* before you speak. Pokey wants one third of a fair market value. He says that this house, with beach frontage, and a tennis court, and a barn, and an orchard, and ten acres of valuable land, is worth at least one hundred and twenty thousand dollars. Minimum . . . Take some cheese, dear.
Barbara	That means forty thousand each.
Mother	At least. *(pause)*
Randy	We can't do it.
Mother	Of course you can't. Nor can I. Nor can Uncle Bill.
Barbara	Did you tell him we can't?
Mother	Of course I did.
Randy	What did he say?
Mother	He said we can. If we sell.

General consternation

	Oh yes. That's what he said. Sell this beautiful place, pay a huge capital gains tax, divide up the furniture, and get out of here, lock, stock, and barrel, so that Pokey can have his money.
Barbara	He doesn't need the money.
Mother	He says he does.
Randy	He's got a good job. He earns more than any of us.
Mother	He wants to leave that job.
Barbara	With the Department of *Justice*?
Mother	He doesn't like it. He says it's unfair.
Randy	Unfair?

Mother	He's upset about Civil Rights. He says the Department of Justice is unfair to Negroes. I don't know. He wants to leave.
Randy	Golly.
Mother	Just the way he left Andover. Just the way he left Yale Law School. Just the way he left two other jobs in the past ten years. Just the way he left *here,* summer after summer . . . *(ironically)* whenever things are unfair . . .
Barbara	Oh Lord.
Mother	And so he says he needs the money to live on. To support Miriam and the children. While he decides what he wants to do. *(long pause)*
Barbara	So what's the solution, Mother?
Mother	I'll tell you what the solution is *not.* The solution is *not* to sell. That is *not* the solution.
Randy	Of course.
Mother	Sell this spot? Which has been in the family for over eighty years? Why there's nothing that can compare to it on the island, in the country, in the world! I mean, look, just look at that view!

> *They all look out*

Pokey loves it here. In his heart of hearts, he loves it. I know it. And he knows it . . . My glass is empty, Randy.

> *Randy jumps up, takes her glass,*
> *and pours her another Bloody Mary*

It's the same old thing, with Pokey. He leaves. But he always comes back. I mean, he's here, isn't he? He's right here. And he wants us all to make a big fuss.

> *Randy gives her her glass*

Thank you, dear . . . Remember when he was little? He'd come storming in, his bag all packed, ready to run away, and we'd all have to coddle him like mad. Remember? All those trips down to the drug store for special ice cream cones? Well that's what he wants now, at thirty-one years old, and I'm afraid we're all going to have to do it . . . Have some more cheese, Jane.

Barbara	Do what, though, Mother?
Mother	Baby him, dear. Butter him up.
Randy	Pokey's kind of a hard guy to butter up, Mother.

Mother	Not if we work hard. First, I think he needs sleep. He's exhausted from the trip. So I think we should persuade him to take a nap, and keep the children very quiet while he does.
Randy	But I asked him to play tennis this afternoon . . .
Barbara	Oh Randy, God!
Mother	Tennis can wait. Next, I think we can all loosen up. Barbara, the children *can* have coca-cola if they want it. He complained about that, and I told the sitter they can.
Barbara	O.K. Fine. Coke with meals. I'll send you the dentist's bills.
Mother	And tonight, after he's had a nap and his favorite meal, I think, we should try to get him to come to the Yacht Club dance.
Barbara	He doesn't want to go, Mother. He says he hates costume parties.
Mother	Nonsense. He's just forgotten what fun it can be. We'll all go together. I've decided to go as my favorite person, Eleanor of Aquitaine, mother of kings and queens. And Uncle Bill is going as the Great Gatsby. Pokey and Miriam can go as them*selves,* I don't care, but they've got to go. He'll be able to sing, and dance, and see all his old friends. So we've all got to coax him to go.
Randy	O.K.
Mother	And finally, I think we should ask him to stay on. As long as he wants. All summer, if he wants. And if he wants the house to himself, he should have it.
Barbara	Mother!
Mother	It's only fair, Barbara.
Barbara	But we've made plans!
Mother	Change them, Barbara. Pokey comes first.
Randy	But maybe he doesn't want to be here any more, Mother.

Pause; She looks at him

Mother	One thing I *know.* One thing I know without a shadow of a doubt. No one, and I mean no one, can live without roots. No one can cut himself off completely from his

background. People are like plants. If they are cut, they last for a while, but then they wither and die. That I know. And that is Pokey's problem. And that we have got to make him realize, before it's too late for all of us. *(pause)* Now. Change the subject. I want a picture of all of us here on this terrace together. Randy, go into the coat closet and get Daddy's old Kodak. And please call Pokey and Miriam.

Randy goes into the house

Barbara	Mother, if Pokey takes August, what'll I do?
Mother	Ssshhh.

Randy's voice is heard calling Pokey
within

Barbara	But I've sublet my apartment, Mother. Where will I go?
Jane	You could stay with us, back at school.
Barbara	But I don't want to do that.
Mother	Ssshhh.

Randy comes back on with the camera and a package wrapped in brown paper

Are they coming?

Randy	In a while. They're reading to their kids.
Mother	In the middle of the *day*?
Randy	Apparently it's their custom.
Mother	Oh . . .
Randy	*(handing her the package)* But he told me to give you this. He says it goes with the house.
Mother	*(holding it, a little nervous)* How nice.
Barbara	Well open it, Mother.
Mother	All right

She opens it slowly. Everyone watches.

Barbara   Look out. It might explode.

Everyone laughs. Finally Mother gets it open

Mother	Why it's . . .
Barbara	*(squealing)* It's the Family *Bi*ble!
Jane	Bible?
Barbara	We called it that. It's Daddy's notebook. Look Randy! *(She takes it from her Mother)* All the old records. *(to Jane)* We thought it was lost, after he died.

	(to Randy) Pokey kept this, too. *(to Mother)* Oh this is a great house-present, Mother!
Mother	*(shaking her head; quietly to herself)* Pokey, Pokey, Pokey.
Barbara	*(thumbing through the book, as Randy looks over her shoulder)* Look. Here's the geneology. All the old names. Ezra, Abigail, Hepsibah . . . Oh, and here's the account of that fabulous woman. That great, great, great, great, GREAT grandmother, who was raped by Indians, and had her stomach slit open. Remember, Mother? When Daddy used to read that? And she hid herself in a hollow tree for three days, and stuffed her guts back in, and was found and sewn up by her husband, and went on to have eight children? . . . Remember, Mother?

Mother nods

Randy	*(flipping pages; looking over Barbara's shoulder)* Hey. Here are all the Ministers. Look at all the Presbyterian ministers.
Barbara	And here's one of their sermons.
Randy	*(reading; laughing)* "Man is conceived in sin and born in travail . . . Seek not for salvation in the vast splendors of our bounteous land . . . the delights of this world have been set as a bait and a snare . . ." *(more seriously)* "Forswear the pleasures of this world . . ." *(pause)*
Barbara	Isn't that *marvelous*? Isn't that marvelous, Mother?

Mother nods, a little grimly.
Barbara continues reading

	Oh, and here come the businessmen. Look at all these inventories. All this money. Look. Daddy estimated all their incomes . . .
Randy	And furniture. And china. And horses. And automobiles . . . Look, even wash cloths are listed. *(to his Mother)* It's all here, Mother.
Mother	*(impatiently)* I know it's all there.
Barbara	*(flipping the pages)* Oh, and now here are the games. All the old scores of all the old family tennis games. Look: in 1952, Mother and Daddy beat you and me 6-3.
Randy	*(taking the book)* Let me see that . . . Well, here's where I beat Pokey 18-16. *(to Jane)* I told you I could beat him.

Barbara   *(reading over his shoulder)* Oh Mother, look *(she takes the book, shows it to her Mother).* In 1958, you and Daddy beat Fred and me, six-love. I remember that. Fred and I were engaged, and he was visiting, and he could hardly hold a raquet. God, he was horrible. Six-love. I should have read the writing on the wall.

Mother   *(infinitely patient)* Do you think we can take pictures, please?

Randy   *(looking over their shoulder)* Look. Here's 1963. Here's where Uncle Bill started to fill in.

Barbara   Because of Daddy's bad heart.

Randy   Let's see. In '63, Mother and Uncle Bill lost to you and me 7-5.

Barbara   I remember. Poor Daddy had to watch.

Randy   *(taking book)* Hey, this isn't right. It says here that in 1964, Pokey beat me by default. That's not right.

Barbara   Oh yes it is. That was the year you threw your raquet at him. And Daddy made you default.

Randy   Oh yeah . . .

Barbara   *(taking the book, flipping through it)* Wow. Here are the sailing races, and the croquet games, and even our report cards from school . . .

Randy   Who won between Pokey and me in '65. *(He tries to take the book)*

Barbara   *(holding onto it)* Wait a minute. Here are my marks from Westover. Look. See? An A in creative writing. I told you I could write.

Randy   *(pulling at the book)* Let me just see the tennis scores. I know I beat Pokey in '68. I'm sure of that.

Barbara   Randy, don't grab!

Randy   I just want to see '68!

> *Mother gets up, comes between them, takes the book, closes it decisively, and puts it on a table*

I just want to see the record for 1968, Mother.

Mother   *(grimly; wheeling on him)* You won't *find* any record for 1968, dear boy. Because in the summer of 1968, your father *died.* Remember. Taking a long swim,

after a big meal, on a hot day, with a bad heart. That's
what happened in 1968. *(she shakes her head, tears in
her eyes)* Oh what does Pokey think he's doing, dragging
all this stuff up? The bathrobe, the watch, and now
that—that stupid, stupid book! What's he trying to do?

Barbara   It shows he cares, Mother.

Mother   Cares? Cares about what? A lot of old names and
dates and statistics.

Randy   These are our roots, Mother.

Mother   Not at all. That's just a long boring list. I used to beg
your father, I used to beg him when he was working
on that thing, I'd say put in the nice things we all did.
Put in some of the things *I* organised. Where is a
description of the blueberry picking, or the trip to
Cuttyhunk, or the singing by the piano, or the time
we all got together and made this terrace, stone by
stone? Where are the real things? Where is the *life*?
I'd beg him to include those things. But he never
would. All he cared about was things you could own,
and count, and pin down. *(she sits down)* Now
PLEASE! Let's take a picture of us all here together,
out here on this terrace, in the sun! *(long pause)*

Randy   *(quietly)* I want a picture of you, Mother.

Mother   You have plenty of me.

Randy   Not alone.

Barbara   He wants a picture of the bride.

Randy   I want a picture of Mother.

Mother   *(touched)* Oh . . . All right.

> *She dries her eyes, folds her hands in her lap,
> puts her heels neatly together, and tries to
> smile*

Randy   *(kneeling; sighing; then looking up)* Gee. You're still
a beautiful woman, Mother.

Barbara   Portrait of a lady.

> *They all look at her. Pause.*

Mother   Oh take the picture. Take it. Before I go to pieces
completely.

> *Randy sights, focuses, takes the picture, as
> Barbara and Jane look on*

Now. Someone. Get Pokey.

Jane   I'll get him.

She hurries into the house.
The sound of a car horn can now be
heard honking far off left.

Barbara *(with a start)* Oh my God. That's for me. *(She starts hurriedly off left)*

Mother Who is it?

Barbara *(glancing defiantly at Randy)* I've—got a golf game, Mother.

Mother What about the picture? What about lunch?

Barbara Too late, Mother. Goodbye. *(She goes off left)*

Mother *(to Randy)* Who is that? Why can't they come up and shake hands? I don't like people sitting in cars and tooting their horns. *(shakes her head)* There goes the family picture.

Jane comes out of the house.

Jane Miriam's made lunch. It's all ready.

Mother Then we should go in. *(She gets up)*

Jane *(to Randy)* And Pokey wants to take you on in tennis, after lunch.

Randy *(eagerly)* You mean I'll take *him* on.

He cuts across his Mother as she moves
toward the house.

Mother Randy!

Randy Oh! Sorry, Mother.

He holds the screen-door open for her.
She goes in, shaking her head. Randy and
Jane follow, as the lights dim.

END OF ACT I

ACT II

SONG:
I Had A Dream, Dear,
 You had one, too.
Mine was the best dream,
 Because it was of you . . .

Come, sweetheart, tell me,
 Now is the time.
You tell me your dream,
 And I'll tell you mine . . .

Early afternoon light. Shadows are just
beginning to appear on the terrace. The
glasses and cheese have been cleared away,
but the watch is still on the table.
Jane sits on the wall, looking pensively out
to sea. From off left, comes the occasional
sound of a tennis game, and at intervals the
sound of children's voices cheering.

After a moment, Barbara comes in from the
left. She sees Jane, stops, straightens her
hair, adjusts her clothes, puts on a bright
smile, and speaks:

Barbara   Hi.

    Jane starts, and turns.

Jane   We didn't expect you back so soon.

Barbara   We only played nine holes. *(laughs; does up a button on*
her blouse) No. He had to get back to work. Lots of
summer construction. *(pause)* People *work* on this
island, if you can believe it. *(pause)* I'm seeing him
again tonight. I'll have to skip the dance.

    The sound of children cheering and
    clapping, off left.

Hey, how come you're not down there watching the
big match? It looked very heated as I came by. Pokey
and Randy dashing around, snorting and puffing away.
And all the children were sitting in a row on the
bench. Like vultures. *(she looks at Jane)* Shouldn't you
be down there, rooting for your man?

Jane   *(quietly; shaking her head)* I'm tired of games. *(Pause)*

Barbara   *(a little uneasily)* Where's Mother? Taking her nap?
                      Jane nods.
            Was she—peeved at me, for ducking out?

Jane   She never mentioned it again.

Barbara   Then she was peeved. *(pause)* Was lunch awful? Was
            there a lot of bickering about the house?

Jane   Not so much . . . I don't know . . . I was talking to
            Miriam.

Barbara   Oh dear. You got stuck with her.

Jane   Not *stuck.* Not stuck at all. I like her.

Barbara   So do we all, so do we all. *(pause)* What did you talk
            about, with Miriam?

Jane   Oh, I don't know . . .

Barbara   Did you talk about the house?

Jane   No.

Barbara   No?

Jane   We never got to that.

Barbara   Well you must at least have broached the subject.

Jane   No. I'm sorry. I didn't. *(pause)*

Barbara   What *did* you talk about, then?

Jane   Oh . . . Life, I guess.

Barbara   *(laughing) Life?* How heady.

Jane   Her life.

Barbara   *Her* life? Does she have one? Does Pokey let her have
            one? *(pause)*

Jane   She's thinking of leaving Pokey.

Barbara   Oh no . . .

Jane   Unless he decides who he is. She said she wanted
            him to come up here this weekend. So he could work
            things out.

Barbara   Work things *out?*

Jane   She said it's like being married to an elastic band.

Barbara   Whatever that means.

Jane   I think it means that he's stretched. Between their
            life. And this.

Barbara	And which way does she want him to go?
Jane	Either way. Otherwise, she says he'll snap. Or she will. *(pause)*
Barbara	I know the feeling.
Jane	So do I. *(pause)*
Barbara	Well what's her way?
Jane	Oh her life sounds wonderful.
Barbara	According to her.
Jane	No really. I think she has a wonderful life.

> Pause. More noise from the tennis game is heard off left.

Barbara	So do you. So do you have a wonderful life.
Jane	Oh I know. *(pause)* But she . . . does more.
Barbara	Such as what?
Jane	She works, for one thing.
Barbara	Busy, busy, busy . . .
Jane	No, she's got a profession. People . . . need her. People count on her. In her work.
Barbara	What does she call herself?
Jane	I don't even know the title. But she helps families that are falling apart.
Barbara	*(bitterly)* Oh I know that type. I've been through that mill. You sit there, pouring out your soul to those ladies, and they smile, and give you a lot of lingo, or else yawn in your face.
Jane	She didn't yawn in mine.

> Pause; more sounds from left

Barbara	Well you help people, too. You're on some hospital board, aren't you?
Jane	It's not the same.
Barbara	Of course it's the same.
Jane	*(shaking her head)* I'm just there. *(pause)* Miriam's getting her Ph.D. That's what she's doing right now. She's upstairs studying for her Ph.D. So she can teach.
Barbara	Oh, Jews always do that. They're frantic about education.

Jane   And she plays the viola.

Barbara   The viola! My, my.

Jane   In a string quartet. Once a week, rain or shine, she
            gets together with three other people, and they play
            Mozart, and Bach, and Vivaldi together, all evening
            long. Oh it sounds like so much *fun,* doing that.

Barbara   Well you sing, Jane.

Jane   I don't sing.

Barbara   You do, too. You sang in the Nightowls at Vassar, and
            I hope you'll sing at the dance tonight. I hope you
            sing Mood Indigo. I love the way you do that.

Jane   *(singing softly)* "You . . . Ain't . . . Been . . . Blue . . . "

Barbara   *(joining her, in harmony)* "No . . . No . . . No . . . "

            They stop.

            See? I'll bet Miriam can't sing that.

            More sounds from the tennis off left.

Jane   She has such a good relationship with her children.

Barbara   What does that *mean?* A good relationship.

Jane   She lets them grow.

Barbara   So do you. You've taught them to ski and play tennis . .

Jane   But it isn't such a—struggle, with Miriam. She doesn't
            make them wear things, or say things, or learn
            things all the time.

Barbara   And as a result they are spoiled little brats.

Jane   They're wonderful.

Barbara   They're fresh, they're grubby, they use foul language . . .

Jane   But they're so . . . open. They were there all during
            lunch with us.

Barbara   Oh I'm sure. Interrupting Mother, debasing the
            conversation, while our children were out playing a
            good healthy game of softball. Where are Pokey's kids
            now?

Jane   Watching TV, I think.

Barbara   You see? Our children don't do that.

Jane   I know it.

Barbara   Because we have rules about TV. I imagine Miriam
            lets them watch it whenever they want.

Jane   She doesn't like rules.

Barbara   Well that's just the trouble. I think Pokey and Miriam
           spend too much time giving in to their children, and
           kow-towing to them, and being around them. I think
           that's unhealthy. Mother says if you do that, you'll
           turn into a child yourself.

Jane   I suppose . . .

                    Pause. A big groan is heard off left.

           But they fight so.

Barbara   Who fights?

Jane   Our children. Yours and mine.

Barbara   All children fight.

Jane   Miriam's don't. They never fight. They traveled
           all night, and they've been up most of the day, and
           they haven't fought at all.

                    *Pause. Then Randy comes in from the
                    left, in his tennis whites, looking hot and
                    sweaty. He looks at the two women, shakes
                    his head, and slumps into a chair.*

Barbara   Well. Who won?

Randy   *(under his breath)* We didn't finish.

Barbara   What do you mean?

Randy   *(shouting)* WE DIDN'T FINISH! *(pause)*

Barbara   *(looking at Jane; with a sigh)* Well. I'm going to go
           butter up Pokey, and get back into Mother's good
           graces. *(indicating Randy)* He's all yours. *(She goes
           out left)*

                    Pause.

Jane   Where's your raquet?

                    No answer from Randy.

           Where's your raquet, Randy?

                    No answer

           Did you throw your raquet at him? *(No answer)*
           Oh Randy . . .

Randy   I didn't throw it at *him.* I threw it into the poison ivy.

Jane   Oh honestly.

Randy   It was a crumby raquet. I hated that goddam raquet.

Jane   In front of the children.

Randy	I apologized. I said, Come on. I'll get another raquet. I'll get Mother's raquet. Come on. Let's finish the game. But he just walked off the court.
Jane	I don't blame him.
Randy	You don't *blame* him? For walking away? In front of all those kids?
Jane	*(shaking her head)* Throwing your raquet . . .
Randy	He walked away from the game!
Jane	Oh Randy . . .
Randy	Listen. You know what I think. I think he came up here just to beat me. I really think that. He's been practicing *up*, you know. Oh sure. He's been playing all winter, at this jazzy club in Washington. I have to coach hockey, but he's had all winter to practice up for me. He still isn't much good, either. He's got all these cuts and lobs and drop shots, but his serve is a laugh . . .

Jane sighs and starts toward the house.

And I could have won, too. It was my serve when he quit. Do you want to know what the score in games was? Do you—

Jane	*(Suddenly wheeling on him at the door)* Oh Randy, I don't care! I don't CARE who beats who! I don't care whether you beat Pokey, or whether Saint Luke's School beats Exeter, or whether the Los Angeles Rams win or lose! I don't care! I don't care about scores or goals or points or batting averages! Really! I don't CARE, Randy! I Just don't give a SHIT! *(she storms into the house).*

Randy stands up, amazed.

Randy	Hey . . . HEY! . . . Hey, WAIT! . . . What's gotten INTO you?

He hurries after her into the house as the lights fade.

SONG:
You can throw a silver dollar
    down on the ground,
And it will roll,
    Because it's round.

A woman never knows what a good man
   she's got,
   Until she turns him down.
So listen, my honey, listen to me,
   I want you to understand,
As a silver dollar goes from hand to hand,
   So a woman goes from man to man,
(Behind the boathouse)
Yes, a woman goes from man to man . . .

*The lights have come up again. It is now
late afternoon. Shadows are longer across the
terrace.*

*Mother has come out of the house.
She carries a small watering-can and shears,
and begins to water the flowers in the window
boxes, deftly snipping off the dead blossoms
and leaves.*

*Barbara comes out of the house, and
stands by the door, watching her.
Mother ignores her, stonily working on
the flowers. Finally:*

Barbara   Mother, I'm sorry I skipped lunch.

Mother   *(blithely)* Oh that's all right. What's lunch? Just a meal. *(she works on the flowers)* Your brother is here for the first time in five years, it's his first meal here, the whole house is at stake—but what's lunch? Do you think you can make it for dinner?

Barbara   *(with a sigh)* Of course, Mother.

Mother   You see I don't know. People come and go around here as if it were Grand Central Station . . . Now the boys aren't speaking because of that stupid tennis . . . I suppose now Pokey won't go to the Yacht Club dance.

Barbara   He doesn't want to go. I've just been talking to him.

Mother   Why not? Because of Randy?

Barbara   Because Uncle Bill is going.

Mother   And did you try to persuade him? Did you defend your Uncle Bill? Did you make even the smallest effort to keep this family together? *(pause)*

Barbara   I'm not going either, Mother.

Mother   Oh fine. That's just fine.

Barbara   Please don't be mad.

Mother   Mad? Who's mad? What makes you think I'm mad?

Barbara   You won't even look at me.

Mother   *(puttering rather violently with the flowers)* Do I
            have to look at you every minute of the day? Do I
            have to stare at you in order for you to exist? *(pause;
            too casually)* Why do you care how I feel anyway? It
            seems to me my opinion counts for very little in your
            life lately. *(pause)*

Barbara   What does that mean?

Mother   I happened to look out my bedroom window, Barbara,
            and see Artie Grieber's truck in our driveway this
            afternoon. *(pause)*

Barbara   *(with a deep sigh)* Here we go.

Mother   I saw you give him that kiss.
                        Barbara walks away.
            That was quite a kiss.
                        Barbara looks out to sea.
            Quite a kiss. To bestow on a yardman.

Barbara   Not a yardman.

Mother   He was the yardman here.

Barbara   He's a builder now.

Mother   Oh I know what he is now. I've seen every tacky
            summer cottage he's put up. *(pause)* And you said you
            had a golf game.

Barbara   I didn't want an argument.

Mother   You've got one now.

Barbara   I know it. *(pause)*

Mother   I suppose that's where you were last night.

Barbara   Yes.

Mother   At least you're discreet about it. I'll say that.

Barbara   Not now. I told him to drive right up to the door. I'm
            glad you saw.

Mother   Well I don't want to see it again. I never liked him.
            Neither did your father. I don't want to see him
            around.

Barbara	It's my life.
Mother	It's my house.
Barbara	Not any more.
Mother	Until September! And I will not have you living here while you engage in a cheap, adulterous relationship with a local married man!
Barbara	He's separated, Mother.
Mother	Because of you?
Barbara	Yes.
Mother	He's leaving his family because of you?
Barbara	Yes. If he can. They're Catholic.
Mother	You hardly know him.
Barbara	I know him very well.
Mother	Years ago.
Barbara	I've known him all along. Every summer.
Mother	While you were married to Fred?
Barbara	Yes.
Mother	Don't tell me this is the reason for your divorce!
Barbara	Yes. Partly. Yes.
Mother	I am appalled!
Barbara	It's true.
Mother	I am simply appalled. To leave Fred for that sly, ambitious, social climbing Artie Griber. I'm appalled.
	(she sits down; pause)
Barbara	I love him, Mother.
Mother	You can't love him.
Barbara	I've loved him since I've known him.
Mother	What? When he was cutting our grass?
Barbara	Even then!
Mother	That's impossible.
Barbara	*(defiantly)* He was the first boy I ever slept with, Mother.
Mother	I won't hear this.
Barbara	That's why I moved into the maid's room. So he could come back at night. Up the backstairs. And we'd meet on the beach.
Mother	I don't want to hear any of this.

Barbara   Well it's true, Mother. And I love him. And I want
           to marry him. *(starting to cry)* And I should have
           married him all along. I never should have married
           Fred.

Mother   Oh Barbara . . .

Barbara   I never liked Fred. I don't like my children.

Mother   Barbara, Barbara . . .

Barbara   You and Daddy made me marry Fred.

Mother   We did no such thing.

Barbara   *(crying)* You did, you did. You brought him
           around. You turned on the charm. You kept saying
           he was Our Kind. You kept saying it. That's what you
           kept saying, Mother. You pushed me into it.

Mother   Stop it, Barbara.

Barbara   He wasn't my kind. Artie is my kind. And I'm going to
           live with him, Mother.

Mother   Not here, you're not.

Barbara   Oh yes. Right here. Because he's going to buy Pokey
           out. And if Randy doesn't like it, he'll buy Randy out.
           He's got all the money he wants, and he's going to put
           in a sea-wall, and winterize this place, and fix it all up,
           and we'll live here all year round. And I'll see him
           summers and winters and days and nights and we're
           going to screw any time we want!

                    Mother slaps her hard across the face.
                    Barbara reels back, then speaks very quietly
                    through her tears.

           Oh Mother, you hypocrite! You hypocrite!
           Pokey just told me you did the same thing with Uncle
           Bill! For years! And Daddy knew it! And that's why he
           finally killed himself!

                    She runs into the house.
                    Mother stands aghast as the lights dim; then
                    She strides into the house as the song
                    comes up.

                    SONG:
                    I'll be down to get you in a taxi, honey
                    Better be ready 'bout half past eight . . .
                    Now, darling, don't be late,

I want to be there
When the band starts playing . . .
Remember when we get there, honey . . .

*The lights come up again, as the music fades.
It is early evening. There is a rosy glow on the
terrace now. Mother's shears and watering can
are still on the table where she left them.*

*After a moment, Randy comes out of the
house. He wears a white, freshly-laundered
Yale football uniform, including the helmet.
He carries a tray full of gin-and-tonic
ingredients. He sets the tray down on the
table, takes off his helmet, and calls toward
the house.*

Randy   *(calling)* Jane? . . . Are you coming out?

*No answer from within the house. He looks
at the tray, looks back toward the house
again.*

I'm having a drink. Won't you join me? I don't want to
drink alone. *(no answer)* Come on. You'll feel better
once you've had a drink.

*Still no answer. He shrugs, looks at the tray,
then begins to fix himself a drink. As he does,
the screen door opens and Jane comes out, in
her costume. It is her debutante dress, long,
all white, perhaps strapless. She also wears
long white gloves, has her hair done in a
fancy way, and looks young and lovely.
Randy turns from making his drink, and
stares at her, enrapt.*

You. Look. Spec-*tacular!*

Jane   *(shaking her head, walking to the wall)* I feel like a
jerk.

Randy   You look as great as the night I met you . . . Better . . .
Even better.

Jane   I feel like a real jerk. *(pause)* I just showed it to
Miriam. She wanted to know why I was going as Little
Bo-Peep. When I told her it was my coming-out dress,
from my coming-out party, she said, "Ah. The Wasp
Bar-Mitzvah."

Randy   What's a Bar Mitzvah?

Jane   I don't even know. I think it's a ceremony where they
          circumcise people.

Randy   *(returning to making the drinks)* That Miriam. I
          wish she'd lay off.

Jane   *(defiantly)* She's wonderful.

Randy   She bugs me.

Jane   I like her one heck of a lot. *(pause)*

Randy   *(looking at her)* I won't argue. You look too great.

          (He starts to mix drinks. Pause)

Jane   *(suddenly)* I don't want to go to the damn dance.

Randy   *(bringing her a drink)* Oh come on.

Jane   I don't. I look like a jerk. And everyone else there will
          look like a jerk. And act like one, too. Last year there
          were at least twenty debutantes or brides, and another
          twenty football players or hockey players or lacrosse
          players and I don't want to go. I don't want to spend
          a sappy evening trotting around the dance floor with
          all those jerks.

                    *Pause. Randy puts down his drink, looks at
                    her carefully*

Randy   So you think all our friends are jerks, huh?

Jane   *(defiantly)* Yes I do. *(pause)*

Randy   Do you think I'm a jerk?

Jane   I think we're both jerks. *(pause)*

Randy   Do you think our children are jerks?

                    *Pause. She turns away from him,
                    looks out to sea.*

Jane   I think they could be. *(she turns back to him)*
          I think they could turn into jerks very easily. *(pause)*

Randy   Who do you think isn't a jerk?

Jane   Oh . . .

Randy   Who? Come on. *(pause)*

Jane   Miriam. Miriam isn't a jerk.

Randy   I knew it. Why?

Jane   She has a better life.

Randy   That kook?

Jane   Sssshhh.

Randy   *(loud)* She's a kook! You want to wander around with
           your boobs bouncing and your hair in your eyes and
           B.O.?

Jane   She doesn't have B.O.

Randy   She smells, my friend. She hasn't even been swimming.
           Smell her some time.

Jane   Sssshhh.

Randy   That's not a better life, pal.

Jane   It is, it is. They do things, they feel things, they know
           what's going on. *(pause)* We don't. We're babies. We
           live on an island, here and at school. What have we
           done with our lives? All we've done is play games.
           We've missed things, Randy. We've really missed
           things. *(pause)*

Randy   You don't like your life.

Jane   No. I've wasted it.

Randy   Do you want to change it?

Jane   Yes.

Randy   Do you want to change—me?

Jane   I don't know. *(pause)*

Randy   Do you still love me? *(pause)*

Jane   I guess . . . I don't know . . .

                   Randy looks at her for a long time

Randy   Wait there.

                   He goes into the house.

                   *Jane waits nervously, eyeing the screen
                   door. She picks up her drink, is about to take
                   a sip, and then shakes her head and defiantly
                   puts it down, untouched. In a moment,
                   music can be heard from within: a Lester
                   Lanin recording: Bright, bouncing songs
                   from musical comedies in the 50's.*

                   Randy comes back out.

           Hear that?
                   She nods, reluctantly.
           Sound familiar?
                   She nods.
                   *He briskly starts clearing a space on the
                   terrace by moving furniture out of the way.*

Remember your party?

Jane   *(impatiently)* Randy—

Randy   Remember your party?

> Jane nods

You were standing between your parents . . . holding a huge bunch of flowers . . .

> *He picks a flower from the window box, holds it out to her. She hesitates, then takes it.*

And I was visiting Bill Butler after the hockey play-offs at Princeton.

Jane   *(ironically)* What was the score?

Randy   Seven to five in overtime . . . *(He catches himself)* Cut it out . . . I remember coming through the line . . . *(he pantomimes bowing and shaking hands)* How do you do? Good evening. *(He reaches Jane, shakes her hand)* Good evening. Would you like to dance?

Jane   *(walking away)* That's not the way it was, Randy. I had to dance with my father first.

Randy   Still . . . Would you like to dance?

> *She turns; He bows very formally.*

Jane   *(reluctantly)* All right.

> *She holds out her arms.*
> *They begin to dance in the waning light around the terrace, avoiding the furniture. Jane is stiff and reluctant at first. Randy tries a dip.*

Randy   Remember this?

Jane   *(smiling)* Mmmm-hmmmm.

> *More dancing. She dances more enthusiastically now.*

Randy   *(trying a fancy break)* I learned this at dancing school.

Jane   So did I.

> *They dance closer after a while, cheek to cheek, occasionally turning.*

Randy   This isn't so bad, is it?

Jane   Mmmm.

Randy   Dancing on a terrace, on an island, in the sunset,
            overlooking the sea . . .

Jane   Mmmm.

Randy   *(turning)* If this is wasting our life, baby, vive le
            wastefulness.

Jane   *(eyes closed)* Ssshhh.

Randy   *(trying another fancy turn)* Do you think Miriam can
            do this?

Jane   Just . . . sshhh.

> *It is almost sunset now. And the sky is
> beginning to turn a deep blue behind the
> house. Randy and Jane, both with eyes
> closed, now dance very close together, very
> sensuously, even though the music continues
> its bouncy beat. Suddenly it groans to a stop,
> as someone has turned off the machine
> within. Randy and Jane stop, still holding
> each other, in a dance position.*

> *Mother comes out of the house. She wears a
> summer jacket dress; with high heels, and a
> small travelling bag. She comes out briskly,
> and speaks very calmly.*

Mother   Randy, I want you to do me a big favor.

> *Randy and Jane stand looking at her,
> amazed.*

            I want you to go down to the beach, Randy, and get
            Pokey, bring him up here, because I want to say
            goodbye.

Randy   Mother . . .

Mother   Just do it, Randy. Right now. Please. Uncle Bill is
            picking me up in ten minutes. We're catching the
            eight o'clock ferry, and we're staying with the
            Robinson's in Boston, and we'll be married—by
            our*selves*—as soon as we possibly can. Go *on*,
            Randy. Please. Get Pokey. The house is yours. There's
            a lamb in the oven and spinach on the stove, and
            you can all fight and argue over dinner all by your-
            selves.

Randy   Mother . . .

Mother   Do it, Randy, before I scream.

> *Pause. He looks at her, sees her determination,
> turns, and angrily goes off right toward the
> beach.*
> *Pause. Mother puts down her bag, looks at
> Jane.*

I. AM. THROUGH. Through with this house, through
with the children, through with the grandchildren,
through with the WHOLE. DAMN. THING. I am free
and clear, as of right now. Take it over, Jane. It's
yours, and anyone else's who wants to pay the taxes,
and plant the flowers, and fix the roof, and order the
meals, and make the gravy, and keep things UP! I've
had it! Count me permanently OUT!

> *Off left, a large bang.*

Jane   *(jumping up)* What's that?

Mother   That was a firecracker! I just gave out all the firecrackers! To all your children! Early! I said, Go
ahead. Let 'er rip. Make as much noise as you want.
This is *my* independence day. Celebrate it, kiddoes!
Make unto the Lord a joyful noise!

> *A string of bangs is heard*

The Mother country is cutting loose from the colonies!
Long live the Queen!

> *Perhaps a Roman candle shoots across the
> dark blue sky; She calls off toward the left.*

Go on! Get hurt! I don't care! Point those things right
at the house! Set it on fire! Who cares? We won't be here,
Bill and I! We'll be off having fun!

> *More firecrackers sound.*

Oh, such spectacular fun! We're going to spend every
nickel we've got. We're going to travel to Europe and
Japan and South America. We're going to get new
clothes and new cars and a new apartment! And I'm
going to forget Christmas, and Easter, and everyone's
birthday, and everyone's size and shape! If someone
gets sick, I don't want to hear! If someone loses a
tooth, or wins a prize, or needs a dress, or wants a toy,
I don't want to know! I don't want to know, I don't

want to hear, I don't want to care! I won't have
anyone's telephone number, and no one will have
mine. I'm unlisted, as of now. If you find me out, I
won't be there. I'm gone, I'm finished, I'm through!

> *More firecrackers; a great barage of
> Roman candles.*

Come on, Bill! Hurry! Take me away! We've got ten
good years to go! Oh boy, oh boy, oh boy! At long
last, we are about to be the most attractive older
couple in the whole, free world!

> *Randy comes on slowly from the right. His
> white Yale football jersey is spotted with
> blood and water. He looks at his Mother.*

Randy   Mother . . .

> *She turns, sees him. Jane moves toward him.*

I hurt Pokey, Mother.

> *They stare at him.*

He—just walked away from me. I tried to tell him, to
come up, but he just walked away. So I . . . I just
picked up this rock and threw it at him. I hit him in
the face . . .

> *Jane gasps and starts off right; Randy
> grabs her arm.*

He's all right. He's bleeding, but he's all right. He's
. . . kneeling in the water. He won't get up. Miriam's
there, and his kids.

> *Jane roughly breaks loose of his grasp and
> runs off right. Mother starts after her.*

Mother . . . MOTHER!

> *Mother stops almost at the exit, her
> back to him.*

He said something about you. About you and Uncle
Bill. That's why I threw the rock. He told a goddam
lie about you.

> *Mother turns and looks at him.*

Mother   Oh sweetheart. *(She goes to him and hugs him)*
Oh my little baby boy.

*Then She turns and walks off right toward
the beach.*

*Randy looks after her. A long string of
firecrackers. Then the lights fade on him.*

*SONG: Sung this time by an individual male
voice, with others humming in the
background:*

O Rose, climb up to her window,
    And into her casement reach . . .
And say what I may not utter,
    In your beautiful silent speech . . .

And then—who can tell? —she may whisper
    While the city sleeps below:
'I was dreaming of him when you woke me,
    But, Rose, he must never know' . . .

*The lights come up again;—it is night. The
terrace is bathed in moonlight. Light also
spills onto it from the windows of the house,
and for the first time, one can see the cosy
rooms inside. The sound of the sea, off right,
can be heard. Mother's suitcase is still where
she left it.*

*Randy sits on the edge of a chair, still
in his bloody football uniform, all
huddled into himself. After a moment,
Barbara comes out of the house. She sees
him.*

Barbara	Nice going.
Randy	*(looking up)* He's all right, isn't he?
Barbara	Oh fine. Fifteen stitches on his forehead. Scarred for life. But fine.
Randy	Can't he have it—fixed?
Barbara	Oh sure he can. But he won't. Not Pokey. He'll wander around for the rest of his life, pointing out his scar, saying, "This is what my brother did. My Wasp brother. Who lost control."

Randy   Is he leaving?

Barbara   I have no idea. He's in his room. With the door closed.
             With Miriam.

Randy   Is Mother leaving?

Barbara   I don't know. Last time I noticed, she was sitting out
             in the car. Talking to Uncle Bill.

Randy   Where's Jane?

Barbara   Putting the kids to bed. Half of them plastered with
             band-aids. They started throwing fire-crackers at each
             other.

Randy   Oh God.

Barbara   It was a pretty explosive evening all around.

                    Pause; He holds his head in his hands.
                    She watches him.

             I assume *you're* leaving.

Randy   I guess so.

Barbara   Oh you booted the ball, Mr. Yale Football player. You
             really did. Any way you slice it, you lose but good. I'll
             bet Mother gives Pokey the house all summer, all by
             himself, and I'll bet he sells it in the fall.

Randy   *(shaking his head)* Oh gee . . .

Barbara   Oh you'll have a lot of money, my stone-throwing
             friend. After a huge tax, why you'll have enough left
             to rent a cottage down here for a couple of years. And
             after that, you can send your kids to a YMCA camp. Or
             why not buy a tent, big enough for all of you? You
             can all huddle together out of the rain and the
             mosquitoes in some trailer park in New Hampshire. I'm
             sure if you drove for twenty miles, you might find a
             public tennis court where you can wait in line to play.

Randy   Quit it, please. Lay off.

Barbara   At least I don't throw large rocks at people when
             their back is turned. *(pause)*

Randy   You lose, too, Barbara.

Barbara   Oh I might be right here, after all.

Randy   What do you mean?

Barbara   Wait and see, kiddo. Just wait and see.

> *Mother comes out of the house.*
> *Both Randy and Barbara stand up*
> *instinctively when they see her.*

Mother   Randy. Go upstairs, and knock on Pokey's door, and
             ask him if he'd please come down here. I want to talk
             to him alone.

> *Randy moves toward the door.*

And don't throw anything at him this time, dear.

> *He turns protestingly.*
> *She waves him out, smiling.*

Go on. Shoo. I know you won't.

> *He exits into the house. Barbara stands*
> *defiantly, facing her Mother. Pause.*
> *Mother speaks very coldly to her.*

Your—truck seems to be parked out in the driveway.

Barbara   *(equally coldly)* Thank you. *(she starts out left)*

Mother   Barbara.

> *Barbara stops, her back to her Mother.*

Ask your friend out there whether he wants you or
this house. Ask him that. Ask him what he'd do if he
can't have the house. Just ask him.

> *Barbara gives her a grim look and exits*
> *quickly.*

> *Mother sighs, sits on the wall, looks out to*
> *sea. She is bathed in a patch of moonlight. A*
> *moment. Then a sound is heard within the*
> *house. She turns toward the door.*

> *A Man appears, a shadowy figure behind the*
> *screen, a shadowed bandage on his head.*

Pokey?

The shadow stands silently; She sighs.

Pokey. *(pause. She looks away from him, speaks out toward the sea)* Pokey, you lied to your brother and sister about me. What you said was not the truth. Do you hear me? I won't ask you to apologize, because I know you won't, but you told a lie, Pokey. *(pause)* And now I'm going to tell *you* something. I'm going to tell you a story. I want you to listen very carefully. I don't want you to squirm and become impatient, as you used to, years ago, when I tried to hold you in my lap. *(pause)* Once upon a time there was a very naive young girl who decided to marry a very upright young man. And at their wedding, she danced with one of his ushers, who had just married someone else. And for a moment, she was carried away. For a moment, she thought, oh dear, have I married the wrong person? And for a moment, the usher thought the same thing. *(pause)* But that was that. She never mentioned it, and neither did the usher, but they knew it, and her husband knew it, and his wife knew it, and they all lived with it, all four of them for thirty-five years. All four were very good sports about it. They played by the rules, and life went on. *(pause)* Do you believe this story, Pokey? I doubt if you do. You never believed the fairy tales I used to tell you. But this one is true. *(pause)* Randy would believe it. And Barbara would too. Oh, she'd say it was very dumb. Very dumb of these people to live this way. And maybe it was dumb. Maybe that's what made your father turn to himself so much, tinkering with his notebook, puttering with the house, swimming all alone. Maybe one day he said to himself, Oh, the heck with it, and kept on swimming out to sea. *(pause)* Now this woman had three children. And the first two seemed very happy, at least for a while. But the third, the youngest, was not. He seemed to sense something wrong almost the day he was born. He'd look at his mother with dark, suspicious eyes, whenever she tried to hold, or feed him, or tell him a story. And as soon as he was old enough, he'd struggle out of her arms. But he'd always crawl back. He'd come, and go. And it went on that way for a long time. *(pause)* Well finally, the woman's husband died, and the usher's wife died, and the two of them thought they might spend their golden years together, sailing into a golden sunset,

with a golden nest-egg between them. But then, at the
last minute, the woman—she was an old woman
now—changed her mind. It was difficult to do, but she
did it. She saw that her two older children had never
grown up. And she blamed herself. And she saw that
her younger son was trying to. And she said to herself,
"I've made my bed, and I must sleep in it. Alone,"
she said. "Alone." *(pause)* So you win, Pokey. I won't
marry Uncle Bill. I'll hold onto this house until the day
I die, according to your father's will. And my children
can come here every summer with their children, and
I'll pay for it, gladly. *(pause)* But you can't come, dear
I'm sorry, but I don't want to see you any more. The
old woman is sending her younger son out to seek his
fortune. I'll try to be as fair as I can at Christmas, and
when I die, but I think we should say goodbye to each
other, once and for all. *(she cries quietly)* I wish you
well, dear. I really do. I think you're an impossible
person, but I love you dearly, and I hope you find
something in life you want to do. I think the best
thing you've done is to marry Miriam and have those
sweet children. I don't understand them, they're out
of my league, but they seem to make you happy,
which is more than I could ever do. *(she takes a
Kleenex out of her skirt; blows her nose; dries her
eyes)* So goodbye, Pokey. I'll get Randy to take you
to the ferry in the morning, and I hope you make it up
with him before you leave. He's a good boy, and he
was trying to defend me. Goodbye, dear.

> *She turns toward the screen, and rises as if
> to kiss him goodbye. But he has gone. She
> whispers to herself.*

Goodbye.

> *Barbara comes in hurriedly from the left.*

Barbara   *(breathlessly)* Mother, what did you mean about
the house? Artie wants to know.

Mother   *(calmly)* I'm keeping the house.

Barbara   Ex*plain* that, Mother.

> *Mother walks away from her*

Mother, he's *wait*ing!

Mother   *(quietly, not looking at her)* Go to bed, Barbara.

> *Barbara looks frantically toward the left,*
> *then toward her Mother. Then she sees*
> *her father's watch still on the table. She picks*
> *up the watch, gives it a futile shake, then goes*
> *with it toward the door. She turns at the*
> *door, and speaks with great resignation.*

Barbara   Goodnight, Mother.

Mother   Goodnight, Barbara.

> *Barbara goes into the house, the watch dangling*
> *from her hand. Randy comes out, now*
> *wearing his father's white bathrobe.*

Randy   Mother, I can't find Jane.

Mother   I think she's sitting on the beach, dear.

Randy   *(beaming)* I knew it! I knew that's where she was!
(He whips off his bathrobe, tosses it onto a chair)
Here. Hold this. *(He runs off toward the right, naked,*
calling) Hey, Jane! Hey, Jane!

Mother   *(calling after him)* Ssshh. You'll wake the children.

> *She stands in the moonlight.*
> *Then she picks up the bathrobe, holding it*
> *limp in her arms, and stands looking out to*
> *sea for a moment.*

> *Then she walks into the house as the lights*
> *fade on her and the screen door slams*
> *behind.*

THE END